See pages 8-13 + 50-74

15
SIMPLE
THINGS
CALIFORNIANS
CAN DO TO
RECYCLE

The EarthWorks Group
&
The California
Department of Conservation's
Division of Recycling

EARTHWORKS PRESS

To Jesse, a special part of the cycle

THIS BOOK IS PRINTED ON RECYCLED PAPER.

Created and packaged by Javnarama
Designed by Javnarama

First Edition 10 9 8 7 6 5 4 3 2 1

The EarthWorks Group has provided a great deal of information
about practices and products in our book. In most cases,
we've relied on advice, recommendations and research
by others whose judgments we consider accurate and
free from bias. However, we can't and don't guarantee
the results. This book offers you a start.
The responsibility for using it
ultimately rests with you.

EarthWorks books are available at quantity discounts
with bulk purchase for educational, business
or sales promotional use.
For information, please contact:
Special Sales Manager
EarthWorks Press
1400 Shattuck Ave., #25
Berkeley, CA 94709
(415) 841-5866

ACKNOWLEDGMENTS

The EarthWorks Group would like to thank everyone who worked with us to make this book possible, including:

- The California Department of Conservation and its Division of Recycling for creating the partnership between government and private industry in an effort to help educate Californians on recycling.

And...

- Edward G. Heidig
- John Javna
- Portia Sinnott
- Fritz Springmeyer
- Ralph Chandler
- Pat Macht
- Stuart Greenbaum
- Marie Felde
- Nicole Magnuson
- Steve Lautze
- Tania Lipschutz
- Lynn Speakman
- Roger Rapoport
- Tania Levy
- Brad Benson
- Deborah Stanger
- Patty Glikbarg
- Gil Friend
- Jay Nitschke
- Recycle America
- Robin Kipke Alkire
- Lenna Lebovich
- Catherine Dee
- John Dollison
- Melanie Foster
- Dayna Macy
- Valentine Paredes

Special thanks to the Board of Directors of the California Grocers Association for their endorsement of this project.

A Note from the EarthWorks Group

We've learned from the success of *50 Simple Things You Can Do to Save the Earth* that people want to know more about how to protect the environment.

Our last book, *The Recycler's Handbook,* provided information on a wide variety of recycling issues. This is a companion volume, specifically targeted to recycling in California.

There is nothing more important than cleaning up our world. But it will be a huge task. It will require the enthusiastic cooperation of every segment of our society—including government and business.

That is why we're so pleased to have joined forces with the Department of Conservation's Division of Recycling and California retailers to bring you this book. We think it is an inspiring example of what can be accomplished when everyone works together.

Recycling is already strong in California. We hope this book contributes to making it stronger.

CONTENTS

A NOTE FROM THE GOVERNOR OF CALIFORNIA

The recycling ethic has taken hold throughout California. The 70 percent recycling rate of aluminum, glass and plastic beverage containers alone signifies that Californians are committed to helping save our environment. Our job is to make sure that you have all the facts to help you participate in this important cause.

This book—a joint venture between the department and the nation's foremost environmental authors—will provide you with all you need to know to become an environmentally responsible citizen. Its quick-reading, to-the-point style will enable you to start saving energy, preserving natural resources and extending the life of our landfills immediately.

Today, California leads the nation as the biggest producer of waste. Together, with your help, California is showing—and will continue to show—its leadership in reducing waste. Recycling plays an important role in solving our solid waste crisis. Your efforts count.

Recycle Today. Save Tomorrow!

Pete Wilson,
Governor of California

RECYCLING

BASICS

Important! Read pgs. 8-13 +
50-74

WHY RECYCLE?

Is recycling really worth the effort? In the end, that's up to you.
But here are a few of the reasons people give for doing it:

THERE'S A GARBAGE GLUT
We've got to do something with all the garbage we create.

• In a lifetime, the average American will throw away 600 times his or her adult weight in garbage. If you add it up, this means that a 150-lb. adult will leave a legacy of 90,000 lbs. of trash for his or her children.

WE'RE RUNNING OUT OF LANDFILL SPACE
Traditionally, we bury most of our garbage in landfills. But land-fills are filling up and closing down all over the country.

• Over the next five years 200 California landfills will close.

• It's happening all over the country. Some 70%, or 14,000, of America's 20,000 landfills closed between 1978 and 1988. By 1993, another 2,000 are expected to close.

SAFETY FIRST
Even if all landfills were available, they'd be health and safety hazards.

• Most landfills were built before safety standards became a high priority. They're not equipped to stop leachate—a toxic liquid that forms in landfill when water combines with decomposing garbage—from seeping into the groundwater.

• How many landfills might eventually leak? According to the Environmental Protection Agency...*all* of them.

THE BURNING ISSUE

Burning garbage isn't the answer either.

• According to Environmental Action, "Even with pollution controls, incinerators are the largest new source of air pollution in most communities....And incinerators produce millions of tons of toxic ash, which still have to go to landfills."

IT'S COMMON SENSE

Making the most of what we've got is an American tradition.

Unlike landfills, which simply stockpile trash, or incineration, which leaves toxic ash to be disposed of, recycling removes waste completely, then turns it back into useful products.

IT'S ECONOMICAL

Recycling is cheaper than landfilling or incineration. You can even make a profit on it.

• Some communities pay more to get rid of their trash than they do to maintain their police departments.

• Recycling saves towns and consumers money. When there's less garbage, we pay less to dump it.

• Individuals and businesses earn money by recycling. One family in Portland, Oregon, picked up enough aluminum cans along roads to pay for air fare to Hawaii. The Boeing Corporation has saved millions of dollars by recycling.

IT SAVES NATURAL RESOURCES

Our resources are finite. If we don't recycle, we'll use them up.

• We can make aluminum from aluminum cans...or from an ore called bauxite. At the rate we're using up bauxite, the Earth will be completely stripped of it in 200-300 years.

• We can use old paper to make new paper...or just keep harvesting trees for virgin pulp. Every day, America cuts down two million trees—but throws away about 42 million newspapers.

• We can re-refine old motor oil to make new motor oil...or keep using virgin oil to produce it. The known oil reserves in the world will only last an estimated 35 years at the rate we're using them.

IT SAVES ENERGY

One of the direct benefits of recycling is energy conservation. For example:

• Every year we save enough energy recycling steel to supply L.A. with nearly a decade's worth of electricity.

• Making one ton of recycled paper uses only about 60% of the energy needed to make a ton of virgin paper.

• We save enough energy by recycling one aluminum can to run a TV set for three hours.

• Recycled glass melts at a lower temperature than new glass, saving up to 32% of the energy needed for production of new glass.

There are indirect benefits to saving energy through recycling, as well. For example:

• By using less energy, we protect pristine land and water from oil drilling.

• Conserving energy reduces pollution from oil refineries.

• America imports about 50% of its oil. Saving energy by recycling means we depend less on foreign supplies.

IT HELPS SAVE THE RAIN FORESTS

We're all concerned about the rainforests. Recycling is a way to do something about it.

• According to *The Rainforest Book*, saving energy through recycling "can reduce the need to construct more dams and power plants for generating electricity. Dam construction in the rainforest accelerates deforestation."

• There's more: "Recycling your newspapers at home as well as white paper at the office will reduce the demand for both tropical and temperate timber."

• Some paper companies find it's cheaper to import paper than make it from U.S. virgin materials. It has been reported that American paper companies import 800 million pounds of paper every year from Brazil.

RECYCLING &
THE ENVIRONMENT

*Here are a few more examples of the way
recycling helps protect the environment.*

THE GREENHOUSE EFFECT

The "greenhouse effect" is caused when gases like carbon dioxide (CO_2) and methane are released into the atmosphere. These gases form a blanket around the Earth which acts like the glass walls of a greenhouse; sunlight can get in, but heat can't get out. When the "blanket keeps getting thicker, the result is global warming.

What Causes It

Carbon dioxide is released when coal, oil and natural gas are burned by power plants, factories and vehicles. Methane gas builds up when garbage decomposes in landfills, and is released upward through the trash.

The Recycling Connection

Recycling saves energy in the manufacturing process (for instance, recycled aluminum needs 95% less energy than aluminum made from raw materials)—so less CO_2 is released.

• Recycling keeps trash out of landfills. Less trash, less gas.

• Trees "eat" CO_2. The more paper we recycle, the fewer trees we cut down. The end result? Cleaner air.

WATER POLLUTION

More than half the people in the U.S. rely on groundwater as their drinking water. But groundwater is becoming polluted.

What Causes It

Hazardous chemicals dumped by factories; used motor oil, antifreeze and paint dumped by consumers; leachate in landfills that has mixed with rain; and more.

The Recycling Connection

Recycling hazardous waste keeps it out of our groundwater.

• Recycling means less leachate to pollute the water.

• Recycling means less industrial waste in the water. Recycling a ton of office paper, for example, keeps 7,000 gallons of water out of the papermaking process. And it cuts down on bleaching, which means less dioxins in the water.

SOIL EROSION

According to one estimate, the U.S. loses enough soil every year to fill 50 million boxcars. When this soil ends up in the water, it harms fish and pollutes our drinking water.

What Causes It

Picture a forest after it's been clearcut. The trees that held the soil in place are gone, so it washes into lakes and streams.

The Recycling Connection

When we reuse paper and wood products, we can cut down fewer trees...so more topsoil stays put.

ACID RAIN

Gases called sulfur oxides and nitrogen oxides mix with moisture in the atmosphere. When the moisture falls as rain or snow, the acidic gases fall with it, damaging crops and forests. In some places, the rain is now as acidic as lemon juice.

What Causes It

The gases are emitted by cars, factories and power plants when they burn fossil fuels (coal, oil and natural gas).

The Recycling Connection

Recycling uses less energy in manufacturing processes, so it reduces the burning of fossil fuels...and acid rain.

WHAT *IS* A RECYCLING CENTER?

All recycling centers are not created equal. There are centers that come to you…and centers you bring your recyclables to; centers staffed with (usually) friendly people…and centers that are just vending machines.

Here's a description of the different types of centers you'll find in California:

CURBSIDE COLLECTION

• This is as easy as it gets; you put recyclable items on the curb on a designated day, and someone comes by to haul them away.

• Most curbside programs accept newspaper, cans and glass bottles. A few take plastic soda bottles, milk jugs, motor oil and mixed paper. There may be a separate program collecting yard waste.

• The curbside advantage: It's easy.

• The disadvantage: Convenience costs; cities and counties often charge each household a recycling surcharge. But it's usually less than $1 a month.

• There are 243 curbside programs operating in California; they serve more than 2 million households.

DROP-OFF CENTERS

• "Drop-Offs" are just that—places you can drop off your recyclables…without being paid. Some are really organized. They have separate bins for lots of different kinds of recyclables and are open for specific hours. They often have on-site employees who can answer questions.

• Some drop-offs are very simple—for example, those big bins in parking lots where you can toss your newspapers. There's no staff, and you can use them any time you want.

• You'll frequently find drop-off centers in grocery store parking lots, at community centers and at churches. Every California landfill is now required to have a drop-off center on site.

• Some drop-offs are seasonal, like Christmas tree and phone book recycling centers.

REDEMPTION CENTERS

• All Californians are served by a a special kind of recycling center called a "Redemption Center." These centers are required by the state and are run by private companies. There are currently more than 2,000 of them.

• Their purpose: To refund the deposit—called the California redemption value—you pay on CA Refund Value beverage cans and bottles.

• Redemption centers must pay at least a nickel for every two cans or bottles marked for deposit, and a nickel for every plastic soda bottle over two liters.

• Some centers are equipped with vending machines only. You put a bottle or can into the machine, and it pays you back on the spot. They're called "Reverse Vending Machines."

BUYBACK CENTERS

• If you want to get paid for your recyclables, go to a buyback center.

• Many buyback centers are also redemption centers. They'll redeem your beverage bottle deposit...and pay you for the scrap value of the cans, too.

- They're usually operated by professional scrap firms, although cities and nonprofit groups also run them.

- Some buybacks service only large volumes or just industrial scrap. They may not be interested in accepting individuals' items.

- Their ability to pay for materials depends on the scrap market. If market prices for glass or corrugated cardboard are low, for example, prices at buybacks will usually drop.

OTHER PLACES

- You may not think of them as recycling centers, but 2nd-hand stores, antique shops, and building material salvage yards are among the most efficient ways to keep materials in use.

- "Junk yards" are, too. They're responsible for recycling more steel (in the form of old car bodies) that any other source.

IT'S THE LAW

A number of laws have been passed in California that encourage all aspects of recycling. Here are some of the highlights.

T HE "BOTTLE BILL"
• After 20 years of debate, the Beverage Container Recycling and Litter Reduction Act (AB 2020) was finally passed in 1986. Its goal: To recycle 80% of the state's beverage containers.

• The containers that fall under the bottle bill are glass bottles, aluminum and steel beverage cans, and PET plastic bottles containing: carbonated soda, mineral water, beer and malt beverages, wine coolers and distilled spirit coolers. In the future, other containers are likely to be added.

How It Works
• Stores charge consumers a deposit when they buy beverages, and pay a "refund value" when empties are returned.

• Consumers pay 2¢ when they buy a beverage in a container and receive 5¢ for every two containers they redeem. Plastic containers over 24 ounces require a 4¢ deposit and return 5¢ at redemption.

Redemption Is At Hand
• To make recycling easy, the bill requires stores to make sure there's a place nearby where consumers can return their containers for payment.

• These are called convenience zones; they must be located within a half mile of every major supermarket, and must be open at least 30 hours a week.

• California's bottle bill doesn't stop with consumers. The law tries to ensure that containers are not just collected, but are actually recycled. It does this by offering financial incentives to recyclers and processors.

COLLECTION:

• The California Integrated Waste Management Act (AB 939) requires cities and counties to reduce solid waste at least 25% by 1995 and 50% by the year 2,000. Every city and county will have to create a solid waste reduction plan that includes composting and curbside pickup. Residential, commercial, industrial and institutional government waste are all included.

• In addition, a household hazardous waste collection program must be established by the end of 1991.

CREDITS:

• AB 1490 collects a processing fee for each glass and plastic bottle sold in California and gives a rebate to manufacturers using recycled glass to make new bottles, or any other glass product, such as tile, insulation, bricks or glasphalt.

ENTERPRISE ZONES:

• Cities can create Recycling Market Enterprise zones where state and local governments attract recycling businesses by streamlining permits, reducing fees and providing low interest loans.

PROCUREMENT:

• In 1977, California passed a law giving preference to recycled-content paper. Local governments must buy recycled if the product is within 5% of the cost of non-recycled paper.

• Laws passed in 1989 give preference to other recycled products, too—plastic, glass, tires and compost. Local governments must choose these products if price and quality are comparable.

• All newspaper publishers and printers must use recycled paper for 25% of their purchases in 1991, if paper is available at comparable price and quality. The figure increases to 50% in the year 2000 if the paper is available.

GETTING

STARTED

1. GET CENTERED

*There are over 2,000 recycling centers in California—
enough to make a shopping mall 15 miles long.*

C an you recycle cat food cans in your area? How about plastic milk jugs? Will someone come and pick up those old newspapers you've been saving...or do you have to take them somewhere yourself?

Before you begin recycling, it's important to find out what options are available in your community. It only takes a few minutes, but it's worth the effort—it saves time, energy and unnecessary frustration.

RECYCLING FACTS

Different recycling centers will accept different materials—even if they're in the same community. What they accept depends on:

•*Who's sponsoring them.* A Reynolds Aluminum center, for instance, takes all kinds of aluminum—even pots and pans.

• *Location.* A recycling center in a supermarket parking lot is limited to small, clean materials; a center in an industrial area can accept a much wider range of items.

• *Their equipment.* If they've got bins, forklifts, balers, etc, it's easier to handle a wider variety—and a larger volume—of items.

• *Special marketing arrangements.* The curbside program in Santa Rosa, for example, accepts plastic milk jugs specifically because Dupont has agreed to buy them.

WHAT CALIFORNIANS CAN DO

Find the Recycling Centers in Your Area:

• **Call your city hall or county offices.** Many now have recycling specialists on their staffs to answer questions. And all city offices will know if curbside pickup is available…or if it's planned in the near future.

• **Some communities offer lists of recycling centers.** San Diego County, for example, runs a hotline and produces an annual guide to all county recycling services. The city of Albany, in Alameda County, even provides a map of local second-hand stores.

• **Look in the phone book.** There's a special listing of local recycling centers in some Pacific Bell directories. It's listed under "Recycling and Environmental Information" in the Community Services section at the front of the Yellow Pages.

Check the Yellow Pages listings under "Recycling" or "Recycling Centers. Other listings to check: "Salvage," "Rubbish," "Second-Hand Dealers," "Junk Dealers," "Scrap Metals," "Paper," and "Plastic, Used" (or any used material).

• **To locate the nearest redemption center** (locations change frequently). Check the blue-and-white sign in the window of any grocery store. For the most up-to-date locations, call the Division of Recycling at 800-332-SAVE. The number is staffed 11am-7pm daily.

• **To locate other recycling centers:** Use the California Waste Management Board's free hotline. They'll also tell you who accepts specific items (e.g., used motor oil or plastic). The number is 800-553-2962. It's staffed weekdays from 7:30am-5:30pm, Mon.-Fri.

Find Out What Materials They Accept:

• Some centers specialize in plastic, paper or metal. Some will only take the most profitable items, like aluminum cans.

• Certified redemption centers must accept beverage containers with the "California Redemption" label.

• Some will take just about anything. If you can find a center that takes a variety of materials, ask for a printed list of what they accept. It can help avoid confusion.

Find Out When They're Open:

• **Drop-offs** may be open 24 hours a day...or one day a week. A buyback may be open 6 days, but closed for lunch.

• **Redemption centers** have to stay open at least 30 hours a week, including at least 5 hours on a weekend or evening. Each certified center must post its hours.

• **Curbside Pickup** is usually once a week, though in some communities it's bi-weekly...or even monthly. Be sure you know the scheduled pickup day in your neighborhood.

2. THE PICK OF THE LITTER

*The San Francisco Zoo once recycled animal manure
and sold it as fertilizer called "Zoo Doo."*

Now that you know where you can recycle in your
community, what are you going to recycle?

Of course, that depends on what you've got... and
what you've got time to do.

If you're just beginning, you may want to experiment with
one material at a time. Maybe aluminum, or newspaper...
whatever's easiest. Remember: It's important to be realistic.
If you try to recycle everything at once, you may never get
started.

If you're already recycling the basic materials, consider
expanding your recycling repertoire.

RECYCLING FACTS

• Home recycling doesn't have to take a lot of time.
According to an EPA study, once it's set up it takes only
around 15 minutes a week.

• California's #1 recycling choice? Aluminum. More of us
recycle it than any other material. Every year, we use 8.3
billion aluminum cans...and recycle over 70% of them. The
national average is only about 60%.

• According to one study, Californians recycle about 1.5
billion glass jars and bottles a year. But we still throw away
almost 1.5 billion of them. All of them are recyclable.

• Right now, paper makes up about 40-45% of California's
residential trash.

WHAT CALIFORNIANS CAN DO

Get to Know Your Trash

• **Do a personal "garbage audit."** The best way to find out what you can recycle is to take a closer look at what you throw away.

• **The simplest method:** Watch what you throw away each day...and look in your garbage cans from time to time. What do you see? What's taking up the most room?

• **For a more accurate study:** Set a week aside for you and your household to do a comprehensive audit. Put a box or bag next to each waste basket in your home. Throw "dry" garbage (bottles, cans, plastic, junk mail, etc.) into the box or bag; "wet" garbage (food waste, paper towels, etc.) goes into the regular trash can.

• **At the end of the week:** Sort all the dry garbage. (Use newspapers or a tarp to sort it on.) How much of it can you recycle in your community?

• **Take a long-term view.** You may not be able to recycle all of it right now, but this should help you decide where to start.

• *Check Your Schedule.* It doesn't matter what you *can* recycle if you can't find the time to take it to a recycling center. So be practical—figure out what you have time for. Make a commitment to recycle just that amount. As recycling becomes a habit, you'll be able to add more to the list.

3. MAKE A PLAN

According to a recent survey, women make the decision to start recycling in California households more often than men do.

W ould you keep your empty bottles in the bathtub? Not likely.
Finding a place to store glass and other recyclables is one of the major issues you'll have to tackle when you're planning to recycle.

But that's an easy one, compared to the Big Question: Whose turn is it to load the car and haul them to the recycling center this time?

If you want to avoid the pitfalls of home recycling, it makes sense to come up with a comprehensive plan in advance.

RECYCLING FACTS

• Most curbside programs don't accept junk mail and other "mixed" paper. So if you're planning to recycle it, you'll probably have to make a special trip.

• If you don't have curbside pickup, you can store bottles and cans as long as necessary before recycling. But newspaper begins deteriorating after about a year.

• You may need to plan extra space for glass storage. California glass mills now require recycling centers to separate glass into three colors—brown, green, and clear. The centers may ask you to sort your glass before bringing it to them.

WHAT CALIFORNIANS CAN DO

Decide on a Recycling Center
Some factors to consider:

• **Convenience**

If you use the center closest to you, or on your regular route, you save energy— both your own and any gasoline you use.

• **Payment**

If money's a motivation, find the center near you that pays the most.

• **Charity**

Watch for a recycling drive, or take your materials to a charity-sponsored drop-off. Many buybacks have an "adopt-a-charity" program; they donate the money paid for your recyclables to a specific charity.

• **Number of Materials Accepted**

This isn't just a convenience issue. Recycling centers which take a variety of recyclables provide the greatest service to your community. Your high-value materials can help keep them in business.

Find Out How to Prepare Recyclables

• **Know what's expected of you**

Every recycling center has its own requirements; it's important to find out the needs of the one you'll be using before you start setting up your home recycling area. This will help you determine how to store the materials and how many containers you need.

• **Sample questions to ask:**
  • Do newspapers have to be tied in bundles?
  • Do you have to sort the glass by colors?
  • Do white and colored paper have to be kept separate?

Decide Who's Doing the Recycling

• If you live alone, that's an easy one. If you don't, you need a plan.

• Try to get everyone in the house involved. Include the kids—they want to be part of the action, too. (And it helps them develop good recycling habits early.)

• Remember: It doesn't matter who does what, as long as everyone knows the plan—and agrees.

A Few Things to Consider:

• Who rinses and stores the containers? Does everyone recycle his or her own materials...or is it one person's job?

• If your newspapers have to be bundled, who does it?

• If you have curbside service, someone will have to carry recyclables out to the street, and bring the empty containers back.

• If you drive to a recycling center, will you take turns?

FOR MORE INFORMATION

The Recycler's Handbook: Simple Things You Can Do, *The most comprehensive, easy to read, how-to guide about recycling available.* To get a copy, check your local bookstore or send $5.95 postpaid to EarthWorks Press, 1400 Shattuck Ave., #25, Berkeley, CA 94709.

4. ON THE HOME FRONT

People in an estimated 83% of California households recycle regularly.

I t's 7 p.m., and dinner's over. There are soda cans on the table...empty bottles and jars on the kitchen counter ...and this morning's newspaper is lying on your bed.

Don't you wish you were set up to recycle?

You could be, without much effort.

RECYCLING FACTS

• **In the San Francisco Bay Area:** In 1990 Elmer Grossman, a Berkeley pediatrician, won $1,250 in the city's annual home recycling contest. Here's his set-up: "We have two garbage containers for different colors of glass and a box for cans in the hall. Newspapers are stacked nearby. Then on recycling pickup day, we tote them out to the curb. It's easy."

• **In Los Angeles:** Fourteen-year-old Liz Banuelos got her family to start recycling in their Los Angeles home after hearing environmental lectures at school. "I thought we should do it," she said. "Now we collect aluminum cans, glass and two-litre plastic bottles. At the side of the kitchen door there's a can—we put them in there. Then when it fills up, we put them in bags in the back. When we get a lot, we take them to the recycling center."

• **In San Diego County:** Marvalene and Stan Staats, who live in the San Diego County town of Vista, were amazed at how easy and effective it is to recycle at home. They began keeping their recyclables in three garage bins. "Every night we put the glass, cans, newspapers and plastics in them," says Marvalene. "It's really very convenient. I do more than I

Marvalene. "It's really very convenient. I do more than I probably have to—but I like to wash all the cans and glass and take the labels off."

• **In Marin County:** One resident with a home office didn't think she could do more than recycle bottles and cans. But she's reduced her garbage from 5 cans per week to 3 by recycling junk mail, cereal boxes, magazines and cardboard at curbside. She also takes plastic bags back to the supermarket and the styrofoam to a local supermarket drop-off. She keeps a large basket for paper and a tiny one for trash in each office room at her home.

WHAT CALIFORNIANS CAN DO

Find a Place to Put It

• There's no one perfect place to store recyclables. It depends on your home and recycling habits.

• Just be sure the spot you pick is convenient. If recycling is hard to do, you're less likely to stick with it.

• If space is really tight, limit your recycling. For example, you may consider recycling just cans or paper.

Storage Tips

• Recyclables accumulate in the kitchen, so that's the most common storage area.

• One good place to keep them: Under the kitchen sink— especially if that's where the wastebasket is. Just by changing your aim, you can recycle instead of throwing away.

• No room under the sink? A nearby porch or broom closet might work.

• Newspapers can be stacked almost anywhere. A cardboard box in the corner of a room or garage works fine. Keep a recycling basket where you open your mail.

• Recycling more than one item? Remember: You don't have to keep all the recyclables in the same place.

Keep It Clean

• Some people don't recycle at home because they think it's messy. But it doesn't have to be. The best way to keep things clean: Keep recyclables from stacking up.

• How? Collect only a day's or week's worth somewhere out of sight (under your sink or in a closet), then transfer items to a larger container outside or in a garage.

• Afraid used jars or cans will attract pests? Just rinse them when you do the dishes, or run them through the dishwasher when you do your regular load. That will keep pests away.

Bins, Boxes, Bags

Now that you have a place to store your recyclables, you need something to put them in.

• **If you have a curbside program**, it probably supplies the containers for you to use. Otherwise, use whatever makes recycling easiest for you.

• **Brown paper** bags are good for crushed cans, plastic bottles, and "mixed" paper. Shopping bags with handles are easiest.

• **Cardboard boxes** are ideal. If you want to get your kids involved, ask them to decorate the boxes. Note: Liquor boxes are generally the sturdiest.

• **Plastic buckets work well.** They're inexpensive and sturdy.

• **Stackable plastic recycling bins** allow you to sort and store different kinds of recyclables at the same time. They also save space. Bonus: They're often made of recycled plastic.

• **Canvas or woven plastic bags** can be hung on hooks in a closet, one for each item you are recycling. The drawback: Watch out for drips.

• **Interested in new kitchen furniture?** Department stores, specialty shops and mail order catalogs offer recycling cabinets. Hardware stores have waste baskets in sizes and shapes to fit your space.

Size Counts

• Whatever container you choose, make sure it's a manageable size. If you have to walk down a flight of steps to your car, you don't want to have to carry a container that's too awkward or heavy.

• Speaking of your car, how big is the trunk? This is important because you'll need containers that fit into your car and lift out easily.

5. SET UP AT WORK

The average office worker throws out about
180 lbs. of high-grade paper every year.

Your desk is piled high with paper again, and your waste basket is full. You can't fit one more "While You Were Out" message into it.

It's the same thing every day. You know you could be recycling all that paper, but you're not sure how.

Fortunately, recycling at work is so easy that you and your co-workers can do it without even putting in any overtime.

RECYCLING FACTS

• **In Hayward:** At the Hayward courtrooms of the Alameda County Superior Court, mountains of legal paperwork are now being recycled. "Before, I would fill my wastebasket two or three times a day just with paper," says Judge Joanne Parrilli. Then recycling barrels were placed around the courthouse. "It was an immediate success. All it took was someone picking up the phone and saying let's do it now."

• **In Anaheim:** The 1,100 employees of the Anaheim Hilton and Towers recycle aluminum cans, glass, cardboard and computer paper. They save the hotel more than $30,000 a year on garbage collection costs. Employees benefit too. A portion of the proceeds goes into the employee's activities fund.

• **In San Francisco:** More than 600 bars, restaurants and hotels participate in a recycling program run by NorCal Waste Systems Inc. The joint effort diverts 400 tons of glass a month from the waste stream. "You have to get everyone involved," explains NorCal's Mike Marsh, "—the waitress, the bartender, the cook. Tell them, 'We are going to do something different.'"

WHAT CALIFORNIANS CAN DO

Focus on Office Paper

• Offices usually start their recycling programs with "white paper"—white stationery, photocopy paper, computer paper, any forms on white paper and white scratch pads.

• What's special about it? It's clean and has long fibers, so it brings the highest price when it's sold. That makes it worth your company's effort to recycle it, and worth a waste paper dealer's effort to pick it up from you.

• To find out how much paper your office generates: The rule of thumb is 1/2 pound per day for each employee. That's 2.5 pounds a week per person.

Find a Hauler

• Before you get started, ask your building manager for help. He or she may already be assisting other offices in your building with recycling programs

• Check with city hall. Many large California cities can assist you in setting up a system and in finding someone to take your paper.

• If neither of those approaches work, look in the Yellow Pages under "Waste Paper" or "Recycling" to get the name of a waste paper dealer who'll agree to come and haul away your paper.

• Be sure to ask:
  • What materials will they take?
  • How much will they pay you for each material (white paper, computer paper, newspaper, etc.)?
  • Will they sign a long-term (i.e. one year) contract?
  • How often will they make pick-ups?
  • Can they supply references?

• Does your company destroy confidential documents? That's important to know because recyclers usually can't accept shredded paper because they can't tell what kind of paper is in it. You may get a price break if you shred and store your recyclable paper separately.

• Most dealers won't agree to pick up anything less than 500 to 1,000 pounds at a time, so you need to know how much waste paper you plan to recycle before contacting them.

• You don't generate enough paper? Talk to other businesses in your building (or nearby) and see if they want to recycle, too. By joining together, you'll generate more material and make it worthwhile for a collector to pick up from you.

• If you still can't get a collector, you can always drop off the materials yourself at a recycling center.

Decide Who's Responsible

• Recycling programs need attention to keep running smoothly, so it's a good idea to have a recycling committee.

• Select one person to act as a liaison among employees, management, janitorial staff and the collectors who pick up your materials.

• Every division or floor (or group of 30 or so employees) should have a recycling coordinator. These people can answer questions and check to make sure people aren't putting trash in the recycling bins.

THE SET-UP

• **The aim is simple:** You want to direct paper that's been going into a trash can into a recycling container instead.

• **Provide a small desktop container to each employee.** This can be a simple cardboard box, or a more elaborate container with separate compartments for different kinds of paper. Some major paper users may need a larger floor box—or you can put one box between two desks.

• **When the desktop box is filled:** Each employee empties it into a larger central container. This can be a barrel, bin or box—but it should be convenient.

● **Station one on each floor,** in hallways or near a photocopy machine. (A lot of paper is discarded there.)

● **One general rule:** Don't make employees walk more than 50 feet to empty their desktop containers. Tests show that if it takes too much effort, they won't do it.

● **Keep it clean.** The success of your program will depend on making sure you get only what you want in the recycling bins. If they're contaminated with other material, the paper dealer won't accept it— and if they pay you at all, will pay you much less.

● **What can you do?** Start by making sure the recycling bin doesn't look like a trash can. Label the bin; if you want only white paper, make sure it says so clearly.

● **When your bins are filled:** They're taken to a central storage/pick-up area. Office recycling programs work best when they're integrated with the trash disposal system. So in many offices, maintenance people simply transfer materials in the central bins to a storage area in the basement or at the loading dock. To be sure: Ask your building manager and the waste paper dealer where they want the material put.

GET THE WORD OUT

At the Start

● Whether your office has three people or 300, everyone needs to know about the recycling program.

● Post a memo before you begin so people know what to expect.

● When you're ready to start, invite everyone to a meeting. Show how the system will work. Explain what can and can't be recycled. A handout helps.

Later

● Let people know if the program is a success. They'll be interested to see what kind of impact their efforts are having.

• In some places, money made through recycling goes into an employee fund, or is donated to charities chosen by employees.

OTHER RECYCLING

• Office paper is the main recyclable at businesses, but you should be able to find someone to pick up bottles, cans, newspapers or other materials if you have enough of them.

• Ask your paper collector if any other materials are accepted; if not, ask for a referral to a company that takes them.

• There's a demand for corrugated cardboard. Grocery stores know this—they've been recycling their boxes for years.

• Many places have vending machines. Take a small step and recycle the aluminum cans. Put a box by the machine for the empties. Offer them to anybody who wants to redeem them. Or let the vending machine supplier haul them away when he comes to restock.

• Look around where you work. You're bound to find something that you can recycle. You'll help keep trash costs down. And you may even make some money.

FOR MORE INFORMATION

• *Your Office Paper Recycling Guide*, San Francisco Recycling Program, Room 271 City Hall, San Francisco, CA 94102. *A wonderful booklet; $5. Make checks out to City and County of San Francisco.*

•The Workplace Recycling Booklet, Division of Recycling, Technical assistance section, 1025 P Street, Sacramento, CA, 95814. *Free guide.*

•*50 Simple things Your Business Can Do to Save the Earth*, EarthWorks Press, 1400 Shattuck Ave, Box 25, Berkeley, CA 94709. $7.95 postpaid, or check your local bookstore.

6. TEACH AN OLD SCHOOL NEW TRICKS

There are more than 350 school recycling programs in Los Angeles alone.

I s your school teaching the 3 Rs?
No, not "Reading, Writing, 'Rithmatic." We mean "Reduce, Reuse, Recycle."

California schools waste a lot of natural resources that could be saved with good recycling programs....The most important of these resources is our children's enthusiasm for protecting the environment. Let's not throw away the opportunity to teach them the value of recycling.

RECYCLING FACTS

• **In the San Francisco Bay Area,** some schools now collect milk and juice cartons to be processed at a new Union City plant called Secondary Fibre Co. When the cartons have been processed, they're sold to another company that recycles them into tissue paper and writing paper. "I want to involve every school in the Bay Area. We can cut their trash bill in half. In a district with 50 or 60 schools, that's a big savings," says the company president Dan Martin.

• **In the San Joaquin County city of Lodi,** the school district's science task force developed a coloring book to teach young children about recycling. Funding was provided by the school's trash company.

• **In Los Angeles:** After a pilot program proved that paper recycling in all of its 600 schools would be easy to implement, the Los Angeles Unified School District moved to develop citywide school recycling programs.

• **At Pleasant Hill Elementary School,** the school-wide recycling program has reduced solid waste by 75 percent. "The janitor used to empty cafeteria trash cans three or four times during lunch. Now, it's done only once, "The supervisor says. The school recycles white paper, newspaper, polystyrene, glass, aluminum, milk cartons and juice boxes.

NOT KIDDING AROUND

• Recycling at schools provides all the usual recycling benefits. It lessens the load on landfills. It reduces the drain on natural resources. And, it can even raise money. But that's not all.

• When children learn how to recycle at school, they don't just stop there. They take it home with them. "I have parents complaining to me all the time that their kids won't let them throw anything away," said Pleasant Hill Elementary School teacher and recycling coordinator, Nan Alexander.

"R" IS FOR RECYCLING

• The recycling lesson should begin before the first scrap of paper or aluminum can is placed into a recycling bin. Students need to learn *why*, not just how, to recycle.

• Even elementary school students can understand that trees are cut down to make their paper. If they recycle paper, they save trees.

• Older students can learn how products are made, what natural resources are used, and how they can be recycled. One school in Bishop has added a "garbage-ology" unit to its junior high school science lesson.

• For instant impact, arrange a field trip to the landfill that handles the students' trash.

• Then show them the alternative: Follow up with a field trip to a recycling center or manufacturing plant that makes products out of recycled material.

• Teach kids about their own garbage—do a garbage audit in

class. Sort garbage during a school week, and figure out how much of it is recyclable.

• Art contests using recyclable items are popular, too. Get local businesses or your city offices to display the winning entries. It will let the kids show their stuff...and teach the community about recycling.

PRACTICE WHAT YOU TEACH

• Once students understand *why* they should recycle, it's easier to get them into the act. Now it's time start a recycling program at your school. There are two ways for schools to recycle: One-time recycling "drives," or ongoing recycling programs.

• One-time drives are excellent fund-raisers for individual classrooms, clubs or PTA's. They raise money by collecting redeemable beverage containers. And ongoing programs make recycling part of every school day.

• Help in setting up a program is available from the technical assistance branch of the State Division of Recycling. Industry groups for plastics, aluminum and glass also make materials available to schools.

GETTING STARTED

• **Form a committee of people interested in recycling.** It should include at least one representative each from teachers, administrators and the custodial staff. It's also helpful to include a student and a parent representative.

• **Your first task:** Decide what to recycle. This depends on what recyclables are generated at the school...and what can be recycled in your area. White paper is always a good bet. So is mixed paper, like construction paper and newsprint.

• **You'll probably be able to recycle aluminum cans** and glass, too—especially if there's a cafeteria.

• **Waste audit:** See what garbage your school generates by emptying a dumpster onto a tarp. Or use the expertise of the people on your committee to estimate what goes into your school's trash.

• **The next job:** Find someone to take your materials. Your local trash hauler is a good place to start. You can also check with commercial recyclers. Look in the Yellow Pages for recyclers or scrap materials dealers.

• **Hauler's choice:** A school can generate enough recyclables to make pickup of many items worthwhile. But what you can recycle will still probably depend on what the hauler is willing to take.

• **One other alternative:** Look around at the recycling businesses in your area. In the San Francisco Bay area, for example, a new recycling company is processing milk and juice cartons. In Los Angeles another is processing polystyrene foam. Both are eager to work with schools to get all the materials they can.

THINK SMALL

• If you live in a rural part of California, have a small school, or don't want to go make a commitment to recycling everything at once, your options may be limited. Don't let that stop you.

• Start small. Try recycling only redeemable cans and bottles. One class or club could make it their project. At Northgate High School in Walnut Creek, the ecology club took it upon themselves to put out recycling barrels for cans and bottles. When the barrels are filled, they borrow a pickup truck and take them to a recycling center. Pretty simple.

GETTING IT TOGETHER

• **Next step:** Once you know what to collect, you have to decide how to collect it.

- **Will each classroom have its own bins for paper?** This works well at many schools. Teachers can assign students to be the "recycling monitor," just as they have blackboard monitors and window monitors.

- **Don't forget the offices,** library and staff rooms. They'll need a way to collect their recyclables too.

- **In the cafeteria:** If you decide to recycle there, set up an assembly line. The first can is for trash. Students dump all the leftover food into it. Next in line are containers for aluminum and glass, followed by a bin for juice and milk cartons and—if you still use them—a place to stack poly-styrene trays.

- **When the recyclables are collected,** you'll have to arrange for them to be brought to a central storage area to await pickup.

- **One easy way:** Have classes alternate in taking responsi-bility for collecting the paper bins from each classroom on their floor or hall. Another is to ask the ecology club or an-other organization step in.

- **If you have a cafeteria program:** You'll need the help of the school's janitors. This shouldn't be a problem—they'll be picking up the same amount of materials; it will just be going into different containers.

- **Once the system is in place:** your school will need a central area to store the collected materials. This could be near the trash dumpster or in another area. Check with the custodial staff and your recycler to find out the best location.

FOLLOWING UP

- **How are you doing?** The kids will want to know. Have someone on the recycling committee work with the recycler to keep track of how much material is being collected. Report back to the students regularly.

- **If your system is making money:** Find a way to let the

kids benefit. Maybe a donation to the PTA for a student project or a special "recycling party."

• **Finally, consider making your recycling part of the community.** If you're already collecting paper, cans and bottles, put out bins so people in the neighborhood use them, too.

FOR MORE INFORMATION
"School Recycling Information Packet," Department of Conservation's Division of Recycling, Technical assistance section, 1025 P Street, Sacramento, CA 95814. *Send for a free guide on starting a recycling program at your school.*

7. A COMPLEX ISSUE

*The 4 million California families who live in apartments
and condos produce an estimated 2 million
tons of garbage every year.*

You've just come home from a garage sale with an old brass lamp and a couple of other items you "just couldn't live without." Now, where are you going to put them? Since you live in an apartment, that's going to be a challenge.

It can be just as challenging to find a place to keep your recyclables. But it can be done—many Californians do it.

RECYCLING FACTS

• **In Los Angeles,** the 4350 Berryman's Homeowners Association tried hard to find a commercial recycler, but there was little interest. So, they found a Girl Scout troop who'd take their materials. "They pick up our cans, PET plastic bottles and glass. It's no more trouble to recycle than to throw out the trash," says the association president.

• **In the city of Los Gatos,** "We'd been doing curbside recycling at single-family homes for a year. The apartment residents kept calling us and asking, 'When can we start recycling?' They really wanted to do it too," said Phil Couchee, with Green Valley Recycling Co. "So we started in January and we are getting close to seven pounds of material a month from every household."

• **In Walnut Creek,** apartment and condo residents are provided a five-gallon bucket for their homes. They place all their recyclables in it and bring it to a central container for weekly pickup. "The recycling ethic is just as strong in multifamily complexes as with people living in single-family homes who must pay their own garbage bill," said the city's assistant city manager.

WHERE CAN STORE RECYCLABLES?

• Many California apartment dwellers keep a box or bin on their outdoor balconies. (Right next to the hibachi.) Other spots: under the sink...or in a closet.

• Really limited space? Try recycling just one item. Crushed aluminum cans take up very little space.

RECYCLING OPTIONS

• If you're lucky, your complex is already part of the wave of new curbside recycling at multi-family buildings. San Diego and Los Angeles are considering starting such programs. San Jose, Davis and Walnut Creek already do it.

• If there's no recycling program where you live, you've got two options: You can find the nearest recycling center and haul bottles and cans there yourself; or you can organize your building into a cooperative recycling program.

• Your city or local recycling organizations may have people ready to help. Call and ask what's available.

FIRST STEPS

• **Meet with your neighbors** and form a committee of interested recyclers. You'll be surprised how many people will be eager to get involved.

• **Contact the building's owner or manager** as a group. If you live in a condominium, talk to the condo association's board of directors.

• **It may help to prepare a handout** on the benefits of recycling. If you don't have time to put together your own, make copies of the "Why Bother Recycling?" section of this book.

• **The most persuasive argument may be the bottom line.** By recycling, you'll reduce the amount of trash that's hauled away; that can add up to substantial savings.

A COMPLEX ISSUE

• Once you have the cooperation of the building manager or owners' association, you can work together to decide how you're going to recycle.

• **The first step:** find someone to haul the recyclables.

• **Your building's trash hauler may pick up your recyclables, too.** If not, you can contact a scrap recycling dealer. Look in the Yellow Pages, or consult other complexes that recycle; ask who takes their materials. A good contact: the local apartment owners and managers' association. Your building manager should know how to reach them.

• Here are some questions to ask prospective recyclers:

  • What materials will they pick up?
  • How often will they pick up?
  • Will they provide central storage containers?
  • What will they pay for recyclables?
  • Will they sign a service contract?
  • Can they provide references?

• **If you can't find a satisfactory hauler:** try contacting nonprofit groups nearby like scout troops or churches. Many are happy to pick up materials—like redeemable beverage containers—that they can make money on.

COLLECTIBLES

• Some private haulers only pick up materials that have a re-sale scrap value, like aluminum and glass. Others may agree to pick up more just to land your business.

• What your apartment building recycles will be determined in part by what your hauler or curbside program agrees to pick up. The most common items are newspaper, glass and aluminum. But you don't have to stop there. For example: In the city of Walnut Creek, a multi-unit curbside program also picks up used motor oil, plastic, tin cans and cardboard.

WHOSE BIN THERE?

• **Most apartment programs** leave it up to individuals to decide how to collect materials in their own units—though some curbside programs do provide containers especially designed for smaller homes.

• **On a building-wide scale:** every apartment house needs a central place to store recyclables until they're picked up.

• **The most common system:** each resident brings his or her recyclables to a central bin.

• **Alternate system:** In large complexes people often put their recyclables in a transfer bin (one is located on each floor). The building maintenance staff then collects them and takes them to a central bin.

• **Check with your building manager or recycler.** He or she may want the central storage bins in a particular place.

• **Typical storage areas:** the basement, a storage shed, parking garage or someplace near the trash dumpster. Remember that some items, particularly newspapers, must be protected from the weather. And make sure the storage area is convenient to both the tenants and the hauler.

• **Storage bins must be clearly distinguishable from the trash bins.** If recyclables get mixed with trash, your recycling service won't accept them.

• **Be sure all containers are clearly marked.** If materials have to be sorted by type, label the bins "newspapers only" or "clear glass only."

• **Note:** At a growing number of apartment houses, all recyclables except paper are put in one bin and sorted by the recycling service. That makes it easier for everyone.

SPREAD THE WORD

• Once you have the logistics of your program down, it's time to let everyone know about it. The best way to reach people is to talk to them in person—a note tacked up on a laundry room bulletin board is less likely to get results.

• You may want to hold a building-wide meeting. Or enlist the recycling committee to go door-to-door to explain the system.

• Along with the personal contact, you should provide a letter explaining when the service will begin, what materials will be accepted, how they should be prepared and where to take them.

• Remember: emphasize that this is a *service* being offered, not a task they're obligated to do.

• Once the program is underway, be sure to update residents from time to time. Tell them how successful the program is. And ask for help in correcting problems—for example, trash being put into recycling bins.

• Share the wealth. Some places use profits generated by programs to hold a party or buy community equipment, like a barbecue. A little payback encourages everyone to keep recycling.

FOR MORE INFORMATION

• **"Strength in Numbers: A Manual for Recycling in Multifamily Housing"**, DEP Office of Recycling, 850 Bear Tavern Rd., Trenton, NJ, 08625. *A wonderful guide for setting up recycling programs in your apartment or condo. Free.*

• *Technical assistance is also available from the Department of Conservation's Division of Recycling.*

MATERIAL

WORLD

8. GLASSIFIED INFORMATION

*Using recycled glass to make new glass cuts
related air pollution by up to 20%.*

T ake a look in your refrigerator. Chances are, there are jars of jelly, mustard, mayonnaise. Plus bottles of soda, beer and the inevitable crusty ketchup bottle.

You've probably got more glass jars and bottles in your house than any other kind of container. And they're almost all recyclable.

According to a recent report, Californians recycle about 56% of the 3 billion glass containers we use every year.

Not bad—but why let the rest of them end up in landfills?

RECYCLING FACTS

• More than 4,000 California restaurants and bars recycle their glass.

• For every ton of glass recycled, we save more than a ton of resources. (1,330 pounds of sand, 433 pounds of soda ash, 433 pounds of limestone and 151 pounds of feldspar.)

• A ton of glass produced from raw materials creates 384 pounds of mining waste. Using 50% recycled glass cuts it by about 75%, to 98 pounds of waste.

• Using recycled glass saves energy. To make glass from raw materials, furnaces must run at 3,500° F. With recycled glass, they run at 2,800° F.

• Glass is easier to recycle in California than in neighboring states. Why? We've got 13 glass plants—compared to one in Oregon and one in Washington.

• One of the most successful refillable bottle recycling programs in the U.S. is Encore, located in Richmond, California. They wash old wine bottles (using a solar-assisted hot water heater) and sell them back to wineries at a lower price than new bottles would cost. The business—a profitable one—employs 15 people and saves 7 million bottles every year.

WHAT CALIFORNIANS CAN DO

Find a Place to Take It

• All California curbside programs and most recycling centers accept glass.

• Redemption centers pay a nickel (or more) for every two beverage bottles with the "CA Redemption Value" on the label. Most redemption centers will take other glass containers, too.

Store It

• It's safer to pack bottles in boxes or bins than in bags.

• Don't leave the bottles in six-pack carriers; that makes extra processing work for recyclers (they have to remove the bottles).

• If you're selling your glass at a buyback center or dropping it off, you'll probably have to separate it into brown, green, and clear glass. The reason: Glass factories need to turn brown glass into brown bottles, green glass into green bottles, etc. If colors are mixed, the end product is an unpredictable hue.

• If you have any blue or other colored glass containers, recycle them with the brown or green glass—but only in small amounts.

• If the glass is even slightly tinted, sort it as colored, not as clear.

• Broken bottles can be recycled; but you may not get paid as much for them as for unbroken bottles.

• Curbside programs generally accept all colors mixed together; only 42 of California's 243 curbside services ask customers to color-sort. The others sort it themselves.

Recycle

• There's no need to take off lids and caps—they're removed at the glass factory.

• It's okay to leave on neck rings, paper and plastic labels—they burn or blow off in the recycling process.

• It's a good idea to dump out food residue and lightly rinse bottles. Old food attracts animals, it's a mess for recyclers, and it stinks. Be sure to empty and rinse beer bottles. A drop of beer can turn into a slimy mold.

• Remove rocks and dirt from bottles found in parks, beaches, etc. One little stone can ruin a whole load of glass.

QUESTIONS & ANSWERS

How is glass recycled?

• Before it's shipped to manufacturers, it's broken so it'll take up less space. This broken glass is called "cullet." When it arrives at the glass factory, cullet is run through a device which removes lids and metal rings from bottles. A vacuum process removes plastic coatings and paper labels. When it's "clean," cullet is added to raw materials and melted down with them in the glass-making process.

What happens to recycled bottles?

They're usually made into new bottles. They're also used in fiberglass or road beds (called "glasphalt").

How many times can glass be recycled?
Glass never wears out—it can be recycled forever.

Is there any glass I can't recycle?
Lots of it. For example, don't try to recycle drinking glasses, light bulbs, safety glass, windshields, mirrors, or Pyrex (baking dishes, coffee pots, etc.) together with glass bottles. Any of these can ruin an entire batch of glass if they slip through at the factory, because they don't melt at the same temperature as bottles.

What about windows?
They *can* be recycled, but only with other windows.

Can I recycle ceramics—like coffee mugs, plates, etc.—with glass?
Absolutely not. They won't melt down with the glass, and will ruin the whole batch.

I hear there's too much glass being recycled in California. Is it true?
No. For a short time there were problems with color-sorting, prices paid for the material, and contaminants. (For example, some bars and restaurants were throwing plates in with their bottles.) But all that's been worked out. The mills can now use all the recycled glass we send them.

What about refillable bottles?
They're the most energy- and material-efficient of all bottles; they can be sterilized and reused until they break, often 15 or more times before recycling. They're not easy to find any more in California, but if you have some, take them back to the store where you purchased them. Note: Some grocery stores now sell milk in deposit bottles again.

SOURCES

"Glass Recycling: Why? How?" The Glass Packaging Institute, 1801 K St. NW, Suite 1105-L, Washington, D.C. 20006. (202) 887-4850.

California Glass Recycling Corporation, 5709 Marconi Ave., Suite C, Carmichael, CA 95608. *Send for information on glass recycling,*

"The Phoenix Project", California Glass Recycling Corporation, 5709 Marconi Ave., Ste. C., Carmichael, CA 95608. *Send for a information packet (limited supply) on starting a glass recycling program in a hotel, bar, or restaurant.*

9. DON'T CAN IT!

*In 1990, Californians recycled an average of
19 million aluminum cans every day.*

For the recycling novice—in other words, almost all of us— aluminum cans are as close to perfect as you can get: No matter how many of them you have, they're still light enough to carry. You don't need any fancy storage containers—you can even pile them into a paper bag. And because aluminum cans are worth so much, you don't have to hunt very far to find someone who'll take them.

The fact is that it's a lot cheaper to recycle aluminum cans than it is to make cans out of new metal. So years ago, the aluminum industry set up collection services, and they've been paying top dollar to get cans back ever since.

If you're wondering where to start recycling, put aluminum cans at the top of your list.

ALUMINATING FACTS
• In 1990, Californians recycled 7 billion aluminum cans.
• The energy we saved was the equivalent of about 850,000 gallons of gasoline *every day*.

• Making cans from recycled aluminum cuts related air pollution by 95%.

• Recycling aluminum also saves 95% of the energy used to make the material from scratch. That means you can make *20* cans out of recycled material with the same energy it takes to make *one* can out of new material.

• According to a recent survey, the average Californian uses as many as three aluminum cans per day.

WHAT CALIFORNIANS CAN DO

Find a Place to Take Them

• Virtually all recycling programs accept aluminum cans.

• Some certified redemption centers will pay at least 70¢ per lb. (that's 28 cans), and many will pay more.

• If you're having trouble finding a recycling center, try the Department of Conservation hotline (800-332-SAVE).

• Check phone listings under "Recycling."

Recycle

• Crushing cans makes storing and transporting them easier. However, reverse vending machines—the automated recycling centers you find at many supermarkets—only accept uncrushed cans.

• It's not necessary to rinse cans...but a large batch of unwashed cans may attract bees and ants.

QUESTIONS & ANSWERS

What happens to our recycled aluminum?

It's compacted into bricks, or baled, then shipped out of state to aluminum smelters, where it's melted down and rolled out into sheet metal. Then it may be shipped back to California, where manufacturers will use it to make more cans.

Can I recycle aluminum foil, too?

Technically, aluminum foil, pie plates, TV dinner trays, etc. are all reusable and recyclable. But in California, foil must be separated from cans because it's made from a different alloy. Curbside recycling programs don't accept it, but all Reynolds Recycling Centers and a number of others do. For information on your nearest Reynolds location, call (800) 228-2525.

What other aluminum can be recycled?

Scrap yards and some recycling centers will take items like window frames, screen doors and lawn furniture. To get the best possible price, remove everything that's not aluminum, like screws, rivets, etc. These centers pay less for "dirty" scrap.

How do I tell if a can is aluminum?

Check it with a magnet; aluminum isn't magnetic. Be sure to check the lids, too—some steel-bodied cans have aluminum tops and bottoms.

FOR MORE INFORMATION

"Aluminum Recycling: America's Environmental Success Story." The Aluminum Association, 900 19th St., NW, Washington, D.C. 20006.

10. POP CULTURE

26 recycled PET bottles equal one polyester suit;
add 3 more and you've got a tie to go with it.

W hen people in the plastics industry talk about PET, they're not referring to Lassie or Mr. Ed. They're talking about *polyethylene terephthalate.*

You may not know the name, but you know the material. In fact, you may have some in your refrigerator right now; PET(or PETE) is what plastic soda bottles and peanut butter jars are made of.

In California, recycling PET / PETE is particularly attractive. Because our state bottle bill requires manufacturers to reimburse recyclers for collecting and shipping the material, we're paid more for PET / PETE bottles than anyone else in the country. So it makes sense to save them.

RE-PETE

• PET bottles account for most of the plastic currently being recycled in the U.S.

• Before California's 1986 bottle bill, almost no PET beverage bottles were recycled. Now we recycle about 31%. That's more than the national average of 25%.

• PET bottles are actually a form of polyester. About a third of all carpeting made in the U.S. has recycled PET bottles in it.

• Other uses: Five recycled PET bottles make enough fiberfill to stuff a ski jacket.

• On average, every California household buys 43 PET bottles a year. That's an estimated 330 million bottles. They could all be recycled.

WHAT CALIFORNIANS CAN DO

Find a Recycler

• For soft drink, wine cooler and mineral water bottles, certified redemption centers are your best bet. They pay 5¢ each for the 2-liter size (which comprise 99% of California's PET bottles).

• Call a local recycling center to find out if they'll take other types of PET bottles—like fruit juice bottles, liquor containers, plastic peanut butter jars, mouthwash bottles, etc. Unfortunately, because there's no state-guaranteed redemption value, there's a good chance you'll strike out.

• Most of California's curbside programs accept PET. You don't have to sort them—just recycle with glass or aluminum cans.

Prepare Bottles & Jars

• Rinse them lightly to keep them from attracting insects.

• Take off the tops, step on the bottles to flatten them (it makes handling and storage easier). If you're using a reverse vending machine, leave them intact.

• Remember: All PET containers are recyclable, including liquor and cooking oil bottles, and peanut butter jars.

QUESTIONS & ANSWERS

How do I tell if it's PET / PETE?

• The easiest way: Look for the number "1" or "PETE" on the bottom of the container, inside the recycling sign. It's part of the standard plastic manufacturer's recycling code.

• PET is usually clear (or clear green).

• On a PET container, there's a small raised dot or nipple—called a *gate*—in the center of the base. On other clear containers (made of vinyl) there's a straight seam, or a "smile," along the bottom. PET bottles never have seams.

Why is PET used for soda bottles?
It's the only plastic that can retain carbonation.

Is it the only plastic used to make beverage bottles?
No. Plastic liquor bottles are always PET, but some imported mineral water is bottled in PVC (vinyl).

Why aren't recycled PET bottles made into new bottles?
According to the Department of Conservation, "PET absorbs chemicals or toxins it is exposed to prior to remelting—and remelting does not remove these absorbed materials." In other words, no one can be sure that a recycled PET bottle is safe for food. Several companies are experimenting with processes that would change this, but they're not currently being used in any products.

What do I do with the caps? And what about the bottoms?
• The caps are generally made of a plastic called polypropylene. Unfortunately, you're not likely to find anyone who accepts it for recycling.

• The bottom cups are a plastic called high-density polyethylene. No need to take them off—they're rinsed in the recycling process and recycled into other products like detergent bottles.

FOR MORE INFORMATION
• **"Pet Projects."** Free newsletter. National Association for Plastic Container Recovery (NAPCOR), 4828 Parkway Plaza Blvd., Suite 260, Charlotte, NC 28217; (800) 762-7267

• **Council for Solid Waste Solutions.** (800) 243-5790. *Call for answers to questions about plastics recycling.*

11. TIN SIMPLE THINGS YOU CAN DO

The energy saved recycling the nation's steel could provide all the electricity for the City of Los Angeles for eight years.

After aluminum, glass and PET, what's next? How about tin and steel cans? You know—the ones pet foods, tomato paste, soup, pork & beans, and other foods come in.

Tin cans are just as easy to melt down and reuse as aluminum, and recycling them can save an incredible amount of resources.

PLAY IT AGAIN, SPAM

• Tin cans are actually 99% steel, with a thin layer of tin added to prevent rusting.

• Californians use over 16 million tin and steel cans every day. We recycle roughly 20% of them.

• At least 70-80% of the tin on a can is saved when you recycle it. This reduces mining waste and preserves a valuable resource.

• Recycling steel and tin cans saves 74% of the energy used to produce them from raw materials.

• Recycling the tin and steel cans used by a California family for a year would save about 125 pounds of iron ore, 20 pounds of coal, and enough energy to light a 60-watt light bulb for more than three months. Not bad for one family.

WHAT CALIFORNIANS CAN DO
Find a Place to Take Them

• California recyclers don't make enough money on tin cans to pay consumers yet, but will often recycle the cans anyway. About one in five curbside programs in California accept tin cans mixed with the aluminum. If yours isn't one of them, contact your local recycling center.

• If you can't find a place, contact the Integrated Waste Management Board hotline at 800-553-2962. Give them your zip code and they'll tell you where to take it.

Store Them

• Store steel cans the same way you store aluminum. But unless your local recycling program instructs you to mix them, keep the two materials separate.

Recycle Them

• If possible, turn the can on its side and step on it to flatten it; flat cans save space for you *and* the recycling truck. (It's easier than it sounds—cans don't have to be perfectly flat.) You might find it helpful to remove the bottom first. If the lids are steel, you can put them inside the flattened can body.

• Empty paint cans—no oil-based paints, please—can also be recycled with tin cans. There can be a layer of paint but it must be dry. Leave the lid off for a while before recycling.

QUESTIONS & ANSWERS
How are tin cans recycled?

They go to "de-tinning" plants, where they're put in wire baskets and lowered into a chemical solution. Then an electric current "zaps" the tin off the cans. Next, the steel is sent to the mills to be reprocessed. In California, there are two processing plants—in Stockton and Los Angeles.

What is the recycled material used for?

The steel can be used in anything from car bodies to nails. It's also used for red, black and yellow paint pigments. Recycled tin is purer than tin made from virgin ore; it's used to make pewter, solder, bronze, bearings—and new tin cans.

Do I have to remove the paper labels?

Not usually. But they wind up as trash in the processing plant, so it might be a good idea to recycle them with mixed paper.

Do I have to wash them out?

Technically, no. But it prevents odors and keeps them from attracting bugs. Suggestion: Put them in the soapy dish water when you're done with the dishes.

How do I know if a can is made of steel?

The easiest way to tell: Use a refrigerator magnet to test it. Steel is magnetic, aluminum isn't. Check the body *and* the lids. (Note: If a can has ribs on the side, it's definitely steel.)

What else, besides food cans, is steel?

The tops and bottoms of cardboard and plastic frozen juice cans, and most jar and bottle lids are steel too. Add them to your can collection.

Can I redeem steel cans, like I do my aluminum cans?

Only if it says "CA Redemption Value" on the lid or label. Then they're worth two for a nickel. Only steel beverage cans are part of the California bottle bill—and fewer than one percent of California beverage cans are actually made of steel.

FOR MORE INFORMATION

• **The Steel Can Recycling Institute,** 680 Anderson Drive, Foster Plaza 10, Pittsburgh, PA 15220. (412) 922-2772.

12. THE PAPER CHASE

Annually, Californians save enough energy by recycling paper to heat 750,000 homes for a year.

If you're one of the millions of Californians who are recycling newspapers, here's some good news: Not only are you saving natural resources and landfill space, you're helping to change the way the paper industry works.

Until recently, newspaper publishers believed that recycling was just a fad—that we'd "get over it." Now that it's clear we're committed to recycling, they're going to expand their use of recycled paper to meet our demand.

The market is opening up for other paper, too. Used paper bags, corrugated cardboard, telephone books, office paper and magazines are being turned into new products every day.

RECYCLING FACTS

• More than 1/3 of the waste stream in California is paper. Almost all that paper could be recycled, but less than 30% is.

• By 1992 every newspaper in California is required to use at least 25% recycled fiber in every edition. That figure will go up to 50% by the year 2000 if the paper is available.

• Some newspapers—like the *Los Angeles Times* and the *Fresno Bee*—are already using a high content of recycled paper. Others use it selectively, saying it doesn't work well with high-speed presses.

• The city of Walnut Creek ran a pilot collection program and found that people have as much "junk mail" to recycle as newspaper. San Jose is getting the same results.

• Most "junk mail" can't be recycled with newspaper, though. It has to be recycled with other odds and ends, called "mixed paper" by recyclers.

• "Mixed paper" is currently being collected in only 18 California curbside programs...but the number is increasing.

• Magazines used to be almost impossible for Californians to recycle. But that's changing, too. Some paper mills on the West Coast are installing new equipment which allows magazines to be mixed in with newsprint during the manufacturing process.

• It's easier to recycle all kinds of paper in California than in other parts of the country, because the Pacific Rim markets will take much of the recycled paper we don't use.

• It's estimated that 70% of corrugated cardboard used in L.A. is recycled. The percentage for the whole state is 55%.

• California has one of the two paper mills in the U.S. that makes newsprint from 100% post-consumer recycled paper.

• We also have mills that make insulation out of newspaper. (Fire-retardant chemicals are added.)

• California recycles more paper than any other state.

WHAT CALIFORNIANS CAN DO

Newspapers

• Ask your recycling center or curbside service if newspapers should be tied or left loose.

• If they need to be tied, put them in bundles about 10 inches thick, so they're easy to carry. Tying tip: Lay the string in a box with the ends draping out over the sides. Put the paper in the box and make the knot.

• If newspapers are to be left loose, store them in brown grocery bags or cardboard boxes.

• Don't worry about pulling out all the glossy inserts, but *don't* add junk mail or magazines to the pile. *Do* keep the paper dry.

• If you're taking the newspaper to a recycling center, you may be asked to empty out the bags or cut the strings holding the bundles; some recyclers prefer just the newspaper.

• Don't recycle newspaper you've used for bird cages or for housebreaking your dog.

Cardboard Boxes

• Recyclers *will* take one box at a time, but it's not really convenient—for them or for you. You'll probably want to store boxes until you've got a bunch.

• First, remove any contents and foreign materials—like foam packing, plastic, string, wire, wood (some boxes are made partly of wood). Then flatten them.

• Don't mix waxed boxes with regular corrugated. The waxed ones aren't recyclable. Once paper fibers are impregnated with wax, they can't be reclaimed.

• Technically, you *can* recycle wet boxes—though not all recyclers will take them.

Office Paper

White Paper

• This is among the most valuable paper to recyclers. It includes: white computer paper, typing paper, stationery (letterhead and bond), notebook and copier paper.

• If you only have a little computer paper, put it in with the white paper. If you've got a lot, keep it separate. It's the highest grade of paper, so you'll get top dollar for it.

• Envelopes with water soluble glue are fine. But plastic windows or adhesive labels may be a problem. Check with your recycler.

• Staples and paper clips are okay. But remove larger metal clips and fasteners (including plastic fasteners).

Other Office Paper

• Generally, it can't be added to the white paper—the fiber has been dyed, and will contaminate the white paper. Check with your recycler to see.

• No construction paper. Add that to your "mixed paper."

• Don't recycle fax paper, NCR paper (carbonless copies), or blueprints; they have chemical coatings.

Magazines

• First choice: Give them to someone else to read. Donate magazines to rest homes, or drop them off at schools for kids.

• Who'll recycle them? Your best bet is a recycling center, but the further you are from a major reprocessing mill, the less likely local recyclers are to accept them.

• Don't mix magazines with any other paper unless your recycling center says it's okay.

• Magazines with staples are fine; the staples are removed magnetically during the recycling process. But magazines with glued bindings, such as *Reader's Digest* and *National Geographic* can gunk up recycling machines. Check with your recycler.

• Get rid of all plastic (even the "biodegradable" kind) before recycling. Some magazines come wrapped in plastic— or have inserts or coupons wrapped in plastic. Subscription cards are okay.

• Glossy junk mail is made of the same kind of paper as magazines, but isn't necessarily recyclable with them. Some mills find it too difficult to check every piece of paper, so they restrict shipments to "magazines only." Check with your local recycler.

Mixed Paper

• It's convenient to store mixed paper in a shopping bag. Since the bag is recyclable, you won't have to empty it.

• Keep all plastics and string out of the mixed paper batch.

• Don't include: fax paper, NCR paper (carbonless carbon paper), wax paper, paper towels, tissues, paper cups and plates.

• Before you recycle junk mail, open and sort through it to take out photos, plastic inserts, and adhesive-backed stickers that may clog machines.

• Envelopes can be recycled; but you may have to rip out plastic windows.

• Glossy stock is ok. In fact, it's preferred by many mills.

• "Paperboard" is ok, including shoeboxes, cereal boxes, toilet paper rolls, cracker boxes, shirt cardboard, etc.

• Remove plastic or wax paper liners in cereal and cracker boxes.

• Egg cartons are the lowest end of the recycling chain, and may already have been recycled. But they can still go to a paperboard mill.

• Reuse wrapping paper if you can. Otherwise, try to pull off most of the tape. Remove string, ribbon, and bows; and be sure you remove mylar or foil.

Bags
• All brown paper bags can be recycled with corrugated cardboard boxes. They're both made of kraft paper.

• White and colored paper bags can be recycled with mixed paper.

QUESTIONS & ANSWERS

What about phone books?

Pacific Bell has pioneered the research to give us the first totally recyclable phone books. They've found a yellow dye that washes out and are using water dispersible glues for the bindings. The covers aren't as shiny because they're coated with a water-based "varnish." But ask at your local recycling center to see if they'll accept old phone books. They may not.

Is it ok to keep my newspapers stacked outside?

Yes, but keep them under cover. Newspapers for recycling have to be kept dry and they shouldn't be exposed to sunlight too long.

How about Manila envelopes?

Most are okay to recycle with mixed paper—but not if they have bubble-pack or foam lining.

Can't I just mix everything together?

Not unless your recycler specifically allows it. Usually you have to separate the newspaper, the mixed paper, the cardboard and the magazines. Follow the guidelines; if you contaminate the supply, your waste paper dealer won't accept it and the whole bunch of it—your paper and everyone else's— will end up in a landfill.

What kinds of paper can't I recycle?

This depends on your recycling center. In general you can't recycle chemically-treated paper like fax paper, blueprints and some copy paper. Some recyclers ask you to avoid anything with adhesives like "Post-it" notes and other stickers. Again, check locally.

FOR MORE INFORMATION

• Contact the American Paper Institute, 260 Madison Ave., New York, NY 10016. (212) 340-0659. *They've got brochures and booklets on recycling everything from paper bags to office paper.*

13. OTHER
MATERIALS

*The used motor oil Californians dump into the environment
each year is the equivalent of more than six Valdez oil spills.*

L ots of different materials—maybe more than you
think—can be recycled. If you're interested in a defini-
tive list, call your local recycling centers, or pick up a
copy of our *Recycler's Handbook*.

In the meantime, here's information on a few more
materials that we think will be interesting to Californians:

PLASTICS

• Many recycling centers in California will only accept
plastic beverage plastic. But that's changing. More plastic is
being recycled.

• Right now, it depends on where you live. Some cities have
pilot programs to collect plastic; some are trying to meet new
waste reduction requirements; some are trying to avoid high
landfill costs. Ask your local recycler.

• There are nearly 50 different kinds of plastics. We
commonly use six of them, but they can't be recycled
together. To make it possible to tell which is which, the
plastics industry is beginning to label them. Look for a
recycling symbol on the bottom of each item, and a number
inside it.

   • 1 is PETE (see page 58).

   • 2 is high-density polyethylene (HDPE). It's used in milk
     jugs, detergent bottles, motor oil containers, etc. Some
     curbside programs and recycling centers now accept it.

   • 3 is polyvinyl chloride (PVC). It's used in credit cards,

shampoo bottles, cooking oil bottles, water bottles, etc. Experts say it has little recycling potential.

- 4 is low-density polyethylene (LDPE). It's used primarily in shrink wrap and plastic bags. Almost all big supermarkets in California accept them for recycling.

- 5 is polypropylene. It's used in plastic bottle caps and lids, drinking straws, yogurt containers, etc.

- 6 is polystyrene and polystyrene foam. It's used for food containers, cups, packing "peanuts," meat trays, etc.

- There's also a #7—mixed plastic, several kinds of plastic mixed or sandwiched together. This is fundamentally unrecyclable. One common use: squeeze bottles.

ORGANICS (COMPOSTING)

• By law, every California city must consider composting as part of their solid waste management programs.

• Since yard waste tends to be at least 20% of California's garbage, it's a great way for your city to reach its mandatory recycling goals.

• Where can you learn to compost? Some recycling centers can help you get started. Garden centers can also help.

• Some cities offer curbside pick up of yard wastes and do the composting themselves. In the city of Davis, residents just rake their leaves into a pile at their curb for pick up. Later they're free to go to the city's compost center and pick up all the compost they want for use in their own gardens.

MOTOR OIL

• By law, Californians must recycle used motor oil.

• But we don't all do it. Of the approximately 137 million gallons we use every year, only half is recaptured.

• Motor oil never wears out—it only gets dirty. Old oil can be re-refined, so it's as good as new.

• How can you recycle it? When you empty the oil from your car, store it in a container that won't leak. (Make sure it has a tight-fitting lid.) Then take it to a recycling center. Some curbside services provide a container for you to use. Over 40 California cities include oil in their curbside programs.

• To find a center that takes used motor oil, call the Integrated Waste Management Board hotline at 800-553-2962.

• Motor oil is considered a hazardous waste, but recycling centers can accept up to 20 gallons from a do-it-yourselfer—in containers that hold five gallons or less—without having to be licensed as hazardous waste disposal sites.

• Don't mix anything in with your oil. It will damage the entire tankful at the recycling center.

HAZARDOUS WASTE

• Hazardous waste can be anything from rat poison to pesticides to spot remover. Many common household items are included. Most cities have printed guidelines which list items considered hazardous waste.

• By law, every California community is required to plan for household hazardous waste collection.

• Some communities have a permanent facility. Others have special collection days for hazardous waste.

• Paint is generally considered a hazardous waste—even latex paint. But a municipality can recycle its latex paint. A Southern California facility mixes it to make a new beige-colored paint. Then they resell it to towns for graffiti removal. The rest is sold commercially as "The Great Coverup" in Standard Brands stores.

• Call the Integrated Waste Management Board hotline, 800-553-2962, for the locations of hazardous waste collections in your area.

14. COMPLETE THE CYCLE

In 1989 there were 170 different recycled products made in the U.S. By 1991, there were more than 2,400 of them.

E ver wonder what's happening to all those cans, bottles and newspapers that people are recycling?

Most are being made into new products. And that's where you come in...again.

To make recycling really work, there must be a market for products made out of recycled materials. You started the chain by collecting recyclable items. Now you can keep it going by buying recycled products. That's called "completing the cycle."

RECYCLING FACTS

• It can take as little as 6 weeks for an aluminum can to be recycled and appear again on supermarket shelves.

• California law requires all glass bottle manufacturers to use at least 15% recycled glass. But plants making beverage containers are already using up to 75%.

• Because California passed a law requiring newspapers to use paper with a minimum 25% recycled content, even Canadian mills—which supply a majority of our newsprint—are expanding their factories to make it possible to use recycled paper.

• California and Maryland had the first programs in the country requiring state government to give a purchasing preference to recycled paper.

• Stores which specialize in recycled products have opened all over California. In the town of Martinez, for example, there's a place called *Turn-around Products.* Their pledge:

"We sell only items made from recycled materials, either recovered or post-consumer."

• If the demand for recycled products grows, businesses will find new ways of using recyclables. New technology to make recycled products will be developed.

WHAT CALIFORNIANS CAN DO

• Make it a priority to buy recycled products whenever possible.

• Ask stores to stock products made of recycled goods. They'll listen, especially if several customers make the same request.

• Write to companies that use recyclables in their products or packaging. Tell them you buy their brand because of it. (Or use the "800" numbers listed on their packaging to call them.)

• If you change brands because your usual one doesn't use recycled materials, write and tell the company whose products you used to buy why you've changed. They'll listen.

QUESTIONS & ANSWERS

How can I tell if what I'm buying is recycled?

• Sometimes it can be hard. More and more, though, it will tell you on the label—especially as regulation of environmental claims gets clearer. California law sets standards for ads on recycled and recyclable products.

What about that symbol with three arrows—does that means it's made from recycled materials?

• Sometimes, but not always. The circle of arrows can mean the product contains recycled materials. Or, it can mean it's recyclable. With paper products, the dark background means it contains recycled fibers.

What can I buy now that's made of recycled goods?

• Aluminum cans and glass containers are almost always made from some recycled materials. So are many brands of paper towels, bathroom tissue and facial tissue. And some paper plates. You can tell by looking at their labels. Some plastic non-food bottles are also made of recycled plastic. Evergreen recycled motor oil will be in stores by the end of 1991.

Is there anywhere to go in California for information?

• Yes, a list of recycled products is being compiled by the Californians Against Waste Foundation. It's part of their new "Buy Recycled" campaign. For a copy, send $2 to their Sacramento offices.

Will buying recycled products cost me more?

• It depends on the product. Items for personal and home use—like stationery and note pads—may cost more because the market for them is still so limited that the cost to produce them is high.

Can anything be done to change that?

• Buy more of them. As the market for recycled products grows, more businesses will get involved and technology will improve. That will make prices come down. Prices for quality recycled office paper are already competitive.

But can I get recycled paper for my office that's professional looking?

• Absolutely. Just ask the attorneys at the big San Francisco law firm of Howard, Rice, Nemerovski, Canady, Robertson and Falk. They use recycled paper for letterhead, second sheets and envelopes. "We looked at the samples and couldn't differentiate," the recycled paper from the virgin paper, says attorney Richard Jacobs.

That sounds good, but where can I find it?

• Ask your own suppliers. If they don't have it, others will. Or call Conservatree Paper Co. in San Francisco, a leader in wholesale recycled paper.

FOR MORE INFORMATION

• **Conservatree Paper Co.,** 10 Lombard St. Suite 250, San Francisco, CA 94111. (415) 433-1000. *Call or write for information about buying recycled paper in large quantities and up to date information about the recycled paper-making processes*

• *The Guide to Recycled Fine Printing and Writing Paper* and *The General Guide to Recycled Products.* Californians Against Waste Foundation, 909 12th St., Suite 201, Sacramento, CA 95814. $3.50 postpaid.

• **"California Market Watch Resource Exchange,"** California Department of Conservation's Division of Recycling, 1025 P St., Room 431 Sacramento, CA 95814. (916) 327-2759. *Provides recycled product info for brokers, equipment suppliers, procurement offices, industry, recycled product manufacturers.*

15. BE AN ACTIVIST

*Nine-year-old Sam Craig organized the "Redio Court
Recycling Club" in his Dublin neighborhood. He and
other neighborhood kids go door-to-door with Sam's
wagon to collect redeemable bottles and cans.
The money they make is theirs to spend.*

All over California, communities are recycling because
someone took responsibility for getting things started.
Whether you want your city to offer curbside recycling
for everyone, or just a convenient place to drop off newspapers, you can make it happen.

SUCCESS STORIES

• The town of Port Costa, at the tip of the Sacramento-San
Joaquin Delta, has its own volunteer community recycling
program. It started when one community member offered to
haul a neighbor's recyclables along with his own to a nearby
town's recycling center.

Lewis Stewart's offer quickly attracted the attention of
others in the tiny community. So he and a friend started
picking up items from neighbors.

As they developed a regular schedule, more people began
to participate. Now, a group of volunteers who call
themselves "Port Costa Recycles" operates a curbside pickup
service on Saturdays. The money they make goes into the
Port Costa Tree Fund to maintain the town's stately elm
trees and to plant new ones.

• The small Humboldt County town of Arcata has a
community recycling center that was started 20 years ago

thanks to the vision of a handful of recycling activists. "At the time, there wasn't any model to go by," said Kate Krebs, one of the founders. "We had to figure it out on our own." Today, the center is thriving—despite the fact it's in a small rural community, far from the major markets for recycled materials.

• In Riverside County, the Lions Club of Hemet runs a 24-hour recycling center. It also operates a fleet of vehicles to pick up recyclables at collection points around the town. It's an effort, but it has its rewards. In eight years the club has made about $200,000.

• A smaller but equally successful program is run by the Belmont Neighborhood Girl Scouts near Los Angeles. The troop picks up cans and bottles from two offices, a church, twenty-four homes and three apartment buildings. "It's the only way we can get money to go on outings to Disneyland and Knotts Berry Farm," explains leader Beth Smart.

NEIGHBORHOOD RECYCLING

• Want to help spread the word? Start in your neighborhood.

• Encouraging recycling in your neighborhood can start by telling your neighbors where the nearest recycling center is. Or take it a step further, and print a simple brochure listing nearby recycling locations. In one California community, the town paid to print up a map of recycling centers.

• If you make a regular run to a recycling center and have extra space in your car, let your neighbors know—maybe you can offer to take an extra bag or box of recyclables with you. Tell them what materials you recycle, and how they should prepare it.

• A one-time neighborhood cleanup can get everyone thinking about recycling. Any money that's made can go to a block party. And if you're successful, regular recycling cleanups could become a neighborhood event.

THE

APPENDIX

RECYCLING HOTLINES

Here are a few numbers to call when you have questions about recycling.

Dept of Conservation Consumer Information Hotline: 800 642-5669. Call for current redemption rates.

Dept of Conservation Redemption Recycling Center Hotline: 800 332-SAVE. For closest recycling centers.

Integrated Waste Management Board Hotline 800 553-CWMB. All-purpose recycling line.

Center for the Development of Recycling . San Jose State University , One Washington Square, San Jose, CA 95192. 800-533-8414. Publications list.

The Environmental Protection Agency National Solid Waste Hotline (National) 800 424-9346

Mobile Recycling Corporation 800 2-MOBILE (Southern California only)

Reynolds Aluminum Hotline 800 228-2525.

Steel Can Recycling Institute Hotline 800 876-SCRI

COUNTY RECYCLING INFORMATION

Want to know more about recycling in your community?
Here's a county-by county, alphabetical listing of
numbers to call, and addresses to write to.

ALAMEDA COUNTY

Alameda County Waste Management Authority
1933 Davis Street, Suite 308
San Leandro, CA 94577
Letters only

The Ecology Center of Berkeley
2530 San Pablo Avenue
Berkeley, CA 94702
415 644-3822

Tri-City Ecology Center
P.O. Box 674
Fremont, CA 94537
415 793-6222

ALPINE COUNTY

Alpine County Recycling Office
P.O. Box 387
Markleeville, CA 96120
916 694-2287

AMADOR COUNTY

Amador County Solid Waste Office
108 Court Street
Jackson, CA 95642
209 223-6546

BUTTE COUNTY

City of Chico
Redevelopment General Services
P.O. Box 3420
Chico, CA 95927
916 895-4800

City of Oroville Recycling Office
2055 Lincoln Street
Oroville, CA 95966
916 538-2480

Butte Environmental Council, Inc
708 Cherry Street
Chico, CA 95928
916 891-6424

CALAVERAS COUNTY

Calaveras County
Department of Public Works
891 Mountain Ranch
San Andreas, CA 95249
209 543-6402

COLUSA COUNTY

Colusa County Department of Public Works
1215 Market Street
Colusa, CA 95932
916 458-5186

CONTRA COSTA COUNTY

Contra Costa County Community Development Dept.
651 Pine Street, 4th Floor, North Wing
Martinez, CA 94553-0095
415 646-4168

West Contra Costa Conservation League
1015 Leneve Place
El Cerrito, CA 94530
415 524-3476

DEL NORTE COUNTY

Del Norte County Department of Public Works
700 Fifth Street
Crescent City, CA 95531
707 464-7229

EL DORADO COUNTY

El Dorado County Environmental Mgmt/Solid Waste
7563 Green Valley Road
Placerville, CA 95667
916 621-5308

FRESNO COUNTY

Fresno County Recycling Office
2220 Tulare Street # 600
Fresno, CA 93721
209 453-5059

GLENN COUNTY

Glenn County Department of Public Works
777 N Colusa Street
Willows, CA 95988
916 934-6530

HUMBOLDT COUNTY

Humboldt County Dept of Environmental Health
529 "I" Street
Eureka, CA 95501
707 445-6215

Northcoast Environmental Center
879 Ninth Street
Arcata, CA 95521
707 822-6918

IMPERIAL COUNTY

Imperial County Solid Waste Dept, Envr Health
Courthouse, 939 Main Street
El Centro, CA 92243
619 339-4203

INYO COUNTY

Inyo County Department of Public Works
P.O. Drawer Q
Independence, CA 93526
619 878-2411

KERN COUNTY

Kern County Solid Waste Management Dept
2700 "M" Street, Suite 500
Bakersfield, CA 93301
805 861-2481 x359

KINGS COUNTY

Kings County Waste Management Authority
280 N Campus Drive
Hanford, CA 93230
209 583-8829

LAKE COUNTY

Lake County Department of Public Works
225 N Forbes Street
Lakeport, CA 95453
707 263-2365

LASSEN COUNTY
Lassen County Recycling Office
707 Nevada St.
Susanville, CA 96130
916 257-8311

LOS ANGELES COUNTY
Los Angeles County Recycling Office
900 S Fremont Ave, 7th Floor
Alhambra, CA 91803
818 458-3563

L.A. County Curbside Recycling Hotline
800 248-9726

Ecology Center of Southern California
P.O. Box 35473
Los Angeles, CA 90035
213 559-9160

MADERA COUNTY
Madera County Environmental Health
135 W Yosemite Ave
Madera, CA 93637
209 675-7823

MARIN COUNTY
Marin County Office of Waste Management
20 N San Pedro Rd, Suite 2002
San Rafael, CA 94903
415 499-6647

MARIPOSA COUNTY
Mariposa County Department of Public Works
4639 Ben Hur Road
Mariposa, CA 95338
209 966-5356

MENDOCINO COUNTY
Mendocino County Department of Public Works
Mendocino County Courthouse
Ukiah, CA 95482
707 463-4363

Ecology Action
5798 Ridgewood Road
Willits, CA 95490
Letters only!

MERCED COUNTY
Merced County Department of Public Works
715 "J" Street, P.O. Box 1391
Merced, CA 95341
209 385-7581

MODOC COUNTY
Modoc County Department of Public Works
202 W 4th Street
Alturas, CA 96101
916 233-3939 x403

MONO COUNTY
Mono County Department of Public Works
P.O. Box 457
Bridgeport, CA 93517
619 932-7911

MONTEREY COUNTY
Monterey County Environmental Health Department
1270 Natividad Road
Salinas, CA 93906
408 755-4511

NAPA COUNTY
Napa County Recycling Office
1195 Third Street #205
Napa, CA 94559
707 253-4471

NEVADA COUNTY
Nevada County Recycling Office
P.O. Box 6100
Nevada City, CA 95959
916 265-1555

ORANGE COUNTY
Orange County Recycling and Resource Recovery Div.
1200 North Main Street, Suite 201
Santa Ana, CA 92701
714 568-4315

Garden Grove Sanitary District
P.O. Box 339
Garden Grove, CA 92642
714 534-3943

PLUMAS COUNTY
Plumas County Department of Public Works
1834 E Main Street
Quincy, CA 95971
916 238-6268

Riverside Waste Mgmt
1995 Market Street
Riverside, CA 92502-1033
714 785-6081

SACRAMENTO COUNTY

Sacramento County Solid Waste Management Division
9700 Goethe Rd Suite E
Sacramento, CA 95827
916 366-2625

Environmental Council of Sacramento, Inc
909 12th Street
Sacramento, CA 95814
916 386-6669

SAN BENITO COUNTY

San Benito County Solid Waste Department
3220 Southside Road
Hollister, CA 95023
408 637-3725

SAN BERNARDINO COUNTY

San Bernardino County Recycling Office
621 E Carnegie, Suite 270
San Bernardino, CA 92415
714 387-0115

SAN DIEGO COUNTY

San Diego County Solid Waste Program
5555 Overland Ave Mailstop 0383
San Diego, CA 92123
619 694-2734

I Love A Clean San Diego
4901 Marina Blvd, Suite 703
San Diego, CA 92117
800 237-2583

SAN FRANCISCO COUNTY
San Francisco Office of Recycling
City Hall, Room 271
San Francisco, CA 94102
415 554-6193

SAN JOAQUIN COUNTY
San Joaquin County Public Works Dept, Solid Waste
P.O. Box 1810
Stockton, CA 95201
209 468-3066

SAN LUIS OBISPO COUNTY
ECOSLO Ecology Center
P.O. Box 1014
San Luis Obispo, CA 93406
805 544-1777

SAN MATEO COUNTY
Peninsula Conservation Center Foundation
2448 Watson Court
Palo Alto, CA 94303
415 494-9301

Common Ground Ecology Center
2225 El Camino Real
Palo Alto, CA 94306
415 328-6752

SANTA BARBARA COUNTY
Recycling Office
123 E Anapumu Street
Santa Barbara, CA 93101
805 568-3055

Community Env. Council, Gildea Resource Center
930 Miramonte Drive
Santa Barbara, CA 93109
805 963-0583 x100

SANTA CLARA COUNTY
Santa Clara County Solid Waste Program
1735 N First Street, Suite 2
San Jose, CA
408 441-1198

SANTA CRUZ COUNTY
Santa Cruz County Planning Dept
701 Ocean, Room 406-E
Santa Cruz, CA 95060
408 425-2721

Ecology Action of Santa Cruz
P.O. Box 1188
Santa Cruz, CA 95061
408 458-1008

SHASTA COUNTY
Shasta County Recycling Office
760 Parkview Ave
Redding, CA 96001
916 225-4420

SIERRA COUNTY
Sierra County Department of Public Works
P.O. Box 98
Downieville, CA 95936
916 289-3201

SISKIYOU COUNTY
Siskiyou County Department of Public Works
305 Butte Street
Yreka, CA 96097
916 842-8250

SOLANO COUNTY
Solano County Planning Dept,
Environmental Mgmt.
601 Texas Street
Fairfield, CA 94533
707 421-6765

SONOMA COUNTY
Sonoma County Department of Public Works
575 Administration Dr, Room 117A
Santa Rosa, CA 95104
707 527-2231

STANISLAUS COUNTY
Stanislaus County Resources Division
1716 Morgan Rd
Modesto, CA 95351
209 525-4160

Ecology Action Educational Institute
1124 13th Street
Modesto, CA 95354
209 576-0739

SUTTER COUNTY
Sutter County Planning Dept
1612 Poole Blvd
Yuba City, CA 95993
916 671-4327

TEHAMA COUNTY
Courthouse Annex, Room I
Red Bluff, CA 96080
916 527-2200

TRINITY COUNTY
Trinity County Department of Public Works
P.O. Box 2490
Weaverville, CA 96093
916 623-1365

TULARE COUNTY
Tulare County Department of Public Works
County Civic Center, Room 10
Visalia, CA 93291
209 733-6409

TUOLUMNE COUNTY
Recycling Office
2 South Green Street
Sonora, CA 95370
209 533-5601

VENTURA COUNTY
Recycling Office
5275 Colt Street #1
Ventrua, CA 93003
805 654-3935

YOLO COUNTY
Recycling Office
292 West Beamer Street
Woodlands, CA 95695
916 666-8775

YUBA COUNTY
Sutter Disposal Company
P.O. Drawer G
Marysville, CA 95901
916 743-6933

MOST-ASKED QUESTIONS

The Department of Conservation's Division of Recycling has put out a flyer listing the most-frequently asked questions about the bottle bill. We've reprinted most of it here.

Q. *What beverage containers can I redeem under the California Beverage Container Recycling Program?*

A. All glass, plastic, and aluminum beverage containers labeled with "California Cash Refund" or "California Redemption Value." Check soda, carbonated mineral water, beer, malt liquor, or wine coolers.

Q. *Do I need to sort my containers?*

A. Yes. Separate the containers by the three material types (aluminum, glass and plastic). Remove the aluminum caps from glass and plastic containers and put them with the aluminum containers. Some centers may want you to separate glass by color.

Q. *How much are eligible containers worth?*

A. The California Beverage Container Recycling Program offers five cents for every two eligible containers under 24 oz. and five cents for each eligible container 24 oz. or larger. Some recyclers also offer scrap value in addition to the regular refund.

Q. *How can I get the most money for recycling?*

A. Find a recycler who pays scrap value in addition to the minimum redemption value of 5¢ for every two containers.

Q. *Instead of taking containers back myself, can I donate them to a worthy organization or charity?*

A. Yes. Many organizations have initiated recycling fund raising drives. Check with your favorite group to see if they're participating. If they are not, suggest that the group contact the Division of Recycling at 1-800-642-5669 to get more information about recycling fund raising opportunities.

Q. *What are the hours of operation of recycling centers?*

A. Recycling centers certified by the State are required to be open for business a minimum of 30 hours per week. Five of those hours must be other than normal business hours.

Q. *Will these centers accept other containers that are not labeled "CA Redemption Value," or other recyclable materials such as newspapers?*

A. Not all recyclers accept and pay for other materials. Certified recyclers MUST accept and pay for labeled glass, plastic and aluminum containers. Shop around until you find the recycler that best meets your recycling needs.

Q. *How can we discourage people from scavenging the recyclables we put on the curb for curbside pickup?*

A. Put your recyclables at the curb just before the collection truck is scheduled for pickup.

Q. *Which plastic containers are eligible for redemption under the California Beverage Recycling Program?*

A. At this point, only soda and carbonated water bottles made from translucent plastic are covered by the program. Eligible containers will be marked with "CA Redemption Value" or "CA Cash Refund."

Q. *What types of glass are accepted in the program?*
A. Glass beverage containers labeled with "CA Redemption Value" or "CA Cash Refund" are accepted. Recycling centers normally don't accept light bulbs, ceramic glass or plate glass because these items consist of different materials than bottles and jars.

Q. *Why doesn't a recycling center take non-California Refund Value glass?*
A. Recyclers are not required to do so. Many will accept them as a donation, however, these containers have not been added to the state's program by the California Legislature.

Q. *Do I have to crush my aluminum cans before recycling them?*
A. No, you aren't required to crush your cans. If you are going to use a reverse vending machine, don't crush them because the machines will not be able to read the bar codes on the cans. However, if you are planning on redeeming your cans at a staffed recycling center, you can crush your cans, as long as one can still read the "CA Refund Value" sign.

Q. *Where can I recycle materials that aren't included in the beverage container program, like cardboard, styrofoam and used oil?*
A. The California Integrated Waste Management Board's Resource Conservation and Recovery Division has a program that includes the recycling of materials such as waste paper and cardboard. Call their toll-free telephone hotline number, 1-800-553-CWMB.

Q. *Who do I talk to if I have a complaint about my recycling center?*
A. If you have a complaint about your nearby certified recycling center, or the beverage container recycling program in

general, just call our toll-free hotline, 1-800-642-KNOW. The operator will forward it to the Division of Recycling Enforcement Branch for investigation. Enforcement staff will investigate your complaint, take the necessary action to remedy the situation, and send you a written report on how the problem was solved.

Q. *What can I do if a reverse vending machine isn't working properly?*
A. If you're having a problem with a reverse vending machine, talk to the store manager about the nature of the problem. If the machine is in need of repair, the manager is responsible for follow-up. While the machine is under repair, the store must redeem your beverage containers. If you find that the machine is not repaired within a reasonable time, please call the Division of Recycling at 1-800-642-KNOW.

Q. *Does my individual effort really help save energy, conserve natural resources and extend the life of our landfills?*
A. Absolutely. The individual efforts of Californians helped the State achieve an overall beverage container recycling rate of 70 percent during 1990. In the last three years, more than 22.2 billion beverage containers have been recycled.